England's Heroes

p

Contents

A Night To Remember:

The Heroes of Munich

Saturday September 1 will be remembered for ever as the night English football inflicted its greatest defeat on Germany. Michael Owen's sensational hat-trick and two more from his Liverpool team-mates Steven Gerrard and Emile Heskey completed the rout.

Stats: September 1, Munich:

Germany 1 (Jancker 6) England 5 (Owen 13, 48, 66, Gerrard 45, Heskey 73.

Half time 1-2. Attendance 63,000.

England's Heroes on the night: Seaman, G. Neville, Campbell, Ferdinand, Ashley Cole, Beckham, Gerrard (sub Hargreaves 78), Scholes (sub Carragher 83), Barmby (sub McManaman 65), Owen, Heskey.

Countdown to the World Cup

By the time the World Cup gets under way, most England fans will have convinced themselves that the title is there for the taking. They will point out that a 10-man team came within an ace of beating Argentina four years ago; and that Sven-Goran Eriksson's men looked world-beaters in the 5-1 demolition job on Germany last September.

David Beckham and European Footballer of the Year, Michael Owen, are undoubtedly the two key players in the squad. Both were there in France four years ago as burgeoning talents; now they are both truly world-class. Steven Gerrard and Paul Scholes are the other two who can lay claim to joining the elite. Should all four be on top of their game in the World Cup, England will be a potent attacking force.

Defensively, it all looks still to play for. Rio Ferdinand, Wes Brown and Sol Campbell are all improving; Ashley Cole is exciting going forward; Gary Neville, Danny Mills and Jamie Carragher may well find themselves vying for the right-back spot. A settled defensive unit will be vital for success, and the time for experimenting is fast running out.

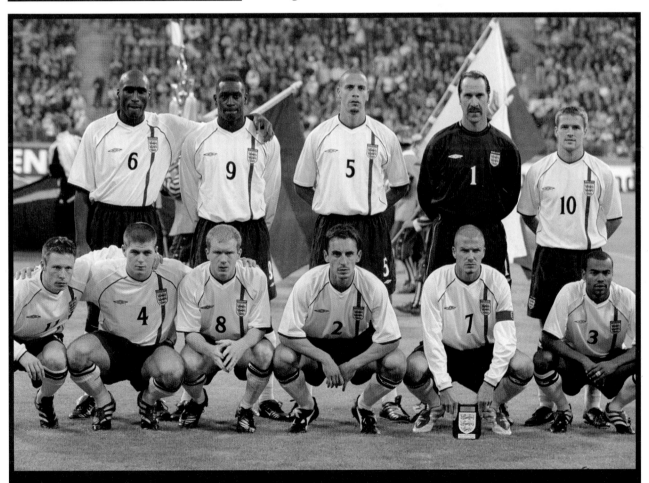

Above: England's victorious qualifiers - Back row, Campbell, Heskey, Ferdinand, Seaman and Owen. Front row, Barmby, Gerrard, Scholes, Neville, Beckham and Cole.

Three Lions Enter

The "Group of Death"

"If England are going to win, they are going to have to do it the hard way"

Not being among the eight seeded teams hit England hard in the draw. The pecking order for the seeding process was based on performances in the last three World Cups, together with current FIFA rankings. Reaching the semi-finals of Italia 90, and the second round in 1998 helped England's cause; but failure to qualify for USA 94 was the critical factor. Even allowing for the fact that England were relegated to the group of second-rank teams, the draw could still have been kinder. Argentina romped through the South America group during qualifying; Nigeria is one of the strongest African sides, and matched England's World Cup performance four years ago; and it is more than thirty years since England recorded a victory over Sweden. There was no other contender for this summer's "Group of Death".

A tough draw for England - but a tough draw for Argentina, Sweden and Nigeria too...

Eriksson was his usual phlegmatic self when the draw was made. There was a shrug of the shoulders, and a quiet determination to get on with the job. The message was clear: it was a tough draw for England - but it was a tough draw for Argentina, Sweden and Nigeria, too. The result against Argentina - England's second opponents - may not be crucial this summer, but the history between the two countries will guarantee the match a massive build-up. England came out on top in an ugly quarter-final encounter in 1966. In 1986, Maradona's two goals - one scored with his hand, the other with his quicksilver feet - won another quarter-final battle for Argentina. And in France four years ago, there was Owen's stunning strike, Beckham's red card, Campbell's disallowed goal and Batty's penalty shoot-out agony. Depending on how the other groups pan out, England could face both France and Brazil in the following rounds, should they win through from Group F. The difficulty of the path mapped out for England at the draw gave rise to one incontestable observation: if England are going to win, they are going to have to do it the hard way.

The England players celebrate the result that put them through to the World Cup 2002.

Path to the Finals

England 0 Germany 1

Finland 0 England 0

England 2 Finland 1

Albania 1 England 3

Greece 0 England 3

Germany 1 England 5

England 2 Albania 0

England 2 Greece 2

Hot-Shot Beckham
sends England to the World Cup finals

David Beckham scores in the first game against Greece in Athens. But it was double trouble for Greece in the second leg at Old Trafford. Who will ever forget the climax of the final World Cup qualifying game on October 6 last year, when one of Beckham's typical stunning free kicks in the dying seconds booked England's place in this year's finals.

David Beckham

Birthplace: Leytonstone 2 May 1975

Height: 5ft 11in

Weight: 10st 8lb

Runner-up to Luis Figo of Portugal as FIFA's 2001 World Player of the Year.

Married to Victoria Beckham July 1999 and has a son, Brooklyn.

David Beckham

England's Captain Marvel

David Beckham made an early mark on the footballing world when he won an award at a Bobby Charlton Soccer Skills school. He had trials with his local club, Leyton Orient, and also attended Spurs' school of excellence. Manchester United then snapped him up as a trainee a couple of months after his 16th birthday. He became an integral part of the celebrated Old Trafford junior side which won the FA Youth Cup in 1993.

Beckham made his debut for United in a Rumbelows Cup match against Brighton in September 1992. But Alex Ferguson was careful to nurture his young star's development. Beckham had to wait until April 1995 for his first Premiership outing. The following season, 1995-96, he established himself as a first choice in United's midfield.

Beckham is acknowledged as the best crosser of a ball in world football

Beckham's rise to prominence came just too late for the Euro 96 party. Glenn Hoddle handed him his first senior international cap in September of that year, in a game against Moldova. He quickly developed into the best attacking midfielder in the country. A playmaker supreme, he sprays inch-perfect, defence-splitting passes all over the field. He is acknowledged as the best crosser of a ball in world football. The wickedly curling balls he whips into the box are a defender's nightmare, but the kind of service that United's front men have thrived on. His dead-ball kicks are legendary, making corners and free-kicks a formidable weapon, both for United and England.

Stunning free kick
In 1999 United achieved a glorious treble, and Beckham's contribution was acknowledged when he was narrowly beaten by Rivaldo for the World Footballer of the Year award. That same year, Beckham married Victoria Adams - Posh Spice - and became a father for the first time. The family man off the field was showing increasing maturity on it. He helped United to win the Premiership in 1999-2000 and 2000-2001, while also being a pivotal player in the World Cup campaign, begun under Kevin Keegan's reign. Beckham's performances for his country have been phenomenal. Who can forget the climax of the game against Greece on October 6 last year, when Beckham's stunning free kick in the dying seconds booked England's place in this year's finals?

Goal of the Season

It was in the opening Premiership fixture of the '96 season that David Beckham scored one of the most spectacular goals ever. Seeing the Wimbledon 'keeper Neil Sullivan off his line, Beckham struck the ball superbly from some 60 yards out. Sullivan was beaten and Beckham had the Goal of the Season sewn up on the opening day.

Along with Michael Owen, Beckham is England's only real world-class player. How he performs this summer will have a major bearing on how far England progresses in the competition.

Owen was just 18 years 59 days when he was awarded his first senior cap for England.

England's youngest international

Michael Owen became the youngest player of the twentieth century to play for the national team, beating the record of one of the famous Manchester Utd Busby Babes, Duncan Edwards. Owen was 124 days younger than Edwards when he made his impressive debut in a friendly against Chile. Less than four months later, he also became the youngest player to score for England when he found the net in a World Cup warm-up match against Morocco.

Terrorising defences

Owen's rise to the top came at the kind of pace that he himself is so noted for. He exploded onto the Premiership scene as a 17-year-old and began terrorising defences and plundering goals right from the word go. He scored on his debut, at Wimbledon on 6 May, 1997, and went on to net 30 goals in the next season, a haul which earned him the 1997-98 PFA Young Player of the Year award.

Michael Owen

England's European Footballer of the Year

Michael Owen turned 22 just before Christmas. He didn't quite manage to notch his landmark 100th goal for Liverpool in time for his birthday. A niggling injury kept him out of the side which went down 4-0 at Stamford Bridge, and he remained on 99 goals from just 181 games for the Reds. There was another very nice present, though: he was named European Footballer of the Year, following in the footsteps of Bobby Charlton, George Best and Kevin Keegan.

The award was no great surprise. Owen had had yet another year filled with electrifying performances, including the brace which snatched the FA Cup away from Arsenal, and that hat-trick in England's 5-1 win in Munich. This goal machine's resolutions for 2002 are simple: to help Liverpool win the league title, then get down to the business of the World Cup, the tournament which launched him to superstar status four years ago.

Owen's memorable strike

It seems hard to imagine now, but Owen went into France 98 as a fringe player. When England fell behind to Romania in their second group match, Glenn Hoddle finally did what the pundits and public alike had been clamouring for. Owen hit the equaliser, and although Chelsea's Dan Petrescu scored an injury-time winner for Romania, Owen had assured himself of a place in the starting line-up. His blistering run and memorable strike in the match against Argentina then confirmed him as one of the stars of the tournament.

The Michael Owen of 2002 is a much better player than the raw talent of four years ago. His first touch has improved markedly, and he is now much stronger on his left foot and in the air. Which is great news for England, not so good for Argentina and the rest.

Michael Owen

Birthplace: Chester 14 December 1979

Height: 5ft 8in

Weight: 10st 9lb

Debut for Liverpool FC in 1997

2001 European Footballer of the Year

Steven Gerrard

England's driving force

Every top side has a driving force in midfield. Roy Keane fills that role superbly for Manchester United, as does Patrick Vieira for Arsenal. In this role Steve Gerrard has been a key player during Liverpool's recent resurgence and a vital cog in Sven-Goran Eriksson's exciting young England team. The fact that he's still just 21 suggests that he could become the best of this brilliant trio of midfielders. Dietmar Hamann thinks he already is, and he is well placed to judge. As well as playing alongside Gerrard for Liverpool, Hamann has also witnessed his trademark crunching tackles, raking passes and deft touches during England-Germany clashes.

Gerrard is a Liverpool lad through and through. He joined the club as an eight-year-old and came through the junior ranks playing alongside Michael Owen. He made his debut in December 1998 and impressed more and more with each subsequent appearance. In some of those early games, competition for midfield places meant that he was played at full-back. With his pace, tenacious tackling and excellent reading of the game, he soon looked the part of an accomplished defender.

It is in the engine room that his aggression, stamina and terrific range of passing come into their own.

But his natural home is in midfield. It is in the engine room that his aggression, stamina and terrific range of passing come into their own. He is a classic box-to-box player, one-minute nullifying an opposition attack, the next setting up a counter with a precision pass or bearing down on goal himself. When he gets within range, he can unleash a fearsome shot. Germany's 'keeper Oliver Kahn found that out during that memorable encounter in Munich last September.

Steve Gerrard has been a key player during Liverpool's recent resurgence and a vital cog in Sven-Goran Eriksson's exciting young England team.

The prospects are mouthwatering; how will the youngster who has taken the Premiership by storm measure up on the biggest stage of all?

Steven
Gerrard

**Birthplace: Whiston
Merseyside 30 May 1980**

Height: 5ft 9in

Weight: 11st 9lb

**England debut: 31.5.2000 v.
Ukraine**

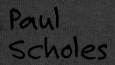

Paul Scholes

Birthplace: Salford, 16 November 1974

Height: 5ft 7in

Weight: 11st 9lb

Joined Manchester United as a trainee July 1991

Married to Claire and has two Children.

Salford-born Scholes joined United as a 16-year-old. He was a member of United's famous Youth Cup-winning side of 1992, the team which spawned so many future stars. He made his Premiership debut in September 1994, against Ipswich Town, and wasted no time in making his mark, scoring both of United's goals in a 3-2 defeat. He finished his first season empty-handed, but since then the silverware has come thick and fast. Last season he picked up his fifth Premiership winners medal; he has also been part of two FA Cup-winning sides. Unfortunately, suspension forced him out of United's famous Champions League Final victory over Bayern Munich in 1999.

England's Jewel

Media-shy, unassuming Paul Scholes may go against the grain in modern football, where the top players are high-profile celebrities as well as athletes. Yet footballing insiders to a man regard him as a jewel of a player. As a classy midfielder with great vision and wonderful technique he is valuable enough. But Scholes also has that special knack for popping up in the box at the right time to score vital goals - a priceless quality.

His international debut came in 1997, against Italy in Le Tournoi de France. Once again, he soon opened his account, grabbing one of the goals in a 2-0 win. By the following summer, France 98, Scholes was an automatic choice for England. He started in all four of England's games and hit a terrific goal in England's 2-0 win against Tunisia.

Scholes the hat-trick hero

A Euro 2000 qualifier against Poland provided Scholes with his greatest moment to date in international football. He grabbed a hat-trick in a 3-1 win and proudly marched off the pitch with the match ball tucked under his arm.

When Kevin Keegan's team stuttered in the Euro 2000 qualifiers and had to face a volatile play-off match against Scotland, it was Scholes who made the difference. He scored both England goals in a 2-0 win at Hampden Park and effectively ended Scotland's hopes of reaching the finals.

Scholes started the all-important World Cup year with 13 goals from 38 England appearances, an excellent return for a midfielder. Even when he scores in the biggest games, Scholes' celebrations are typically understated. Cupping a hand to his ear as though straining to hear the fans' applause counts as a flamboyant display from this nuggety gem of a player.

Paul also has that special knack for popping up in the box at the right time to score vital goals.

Rio Ferdinand

Rio Ferdinand

Birthplace: Peckham, 7 November 1978

Height: 6ft 2in Weight: 11st 13lb

England debut: 15.11.97 against Cameroon

18 million pound bargain

When you pay a world record fee for a player, you might expect to be buying the finished article, not merely exciting potential. Yet when Rio Ferdinand moved from West Ham to Leeds for £18 million in November 2000, there were pundits who said he still had much to learn about the defender's art. A year on, most commentators now think David O'Leary got a bargain.

Excellent ball skills

In the modern game, where counter-attacking plays such an important part, it is a great advantage to have defenders who can get forward. Ferdinand has excellent ball skills; he is comfortable in possession, his distribution is extremely good and he is always a threat from set pieces.

Ferdinand's international call-up came against Cameroon in November 1997, when he had just turned 19. He made Glenn Hoddle's squad for France '98, and although he didn't feature in any of the games, it was experience which could only be of benefit.

Japan and Korea 2002 thus represents the first opportunity for Ferdinand to show his worth on a big stage. Barring injury, he will certainly go into the tournament as first-choice centre-back. It is a tribute to the way he has come on over the past year that the burning question seems to be: "Who should play alongside Ferdinand at the heart of England's defence?"

Ferdinand is hailed as the future for England's central defence for the next decade.

Sol Campbell

Sol Campbell

Name: Campbell, Sulzeer (Sol) Jeremiah

Birthplace: Newham, 18 September 1974

Height 6ft 2in   Weight 14st 4lb

England debut v. Hungary 1996.

Commanding centre half

In recent years, Sol Campbell's international career has provided him with welcome relief from the grind of playing in a Spurs side struggling to rise above mid-table mediocrity. He missed out on the 1991 FA Cup Final victory - he didn't make his debut until the following year - so the only success during his time as a first-team player was a Coca-Cola Cup win over Leicester City in 1999. For a fiercely ambitious player such as Campbell, that was never going to be enough. The decision to move to Arsenal was a controversial one, but 27-year-old Campbell braved the taunts to become a key part of Arsene Wenger's rebuilding job in the Arsenal defence.

Eye-catching forays upfield

Campbell was a towering presence at the back in the last World Cup, and also made some eye-catching forays upfield. He thought he'd put England into the quarter-final when he powered in a header against Argentina, only for the goal to be ruled out for a foul by Shearer.

At the beginning of this season, Campbell took a while to adjust to his new north London home. A turning point came when he returned to White Hart Lane for the first time in an Arsenal shirt. He had an excellent game, despite being on the receiving end of some terrible abuse from the fans who once idolised him.

Despite such performances, Campbell is no longer a certainty for a place in an England starting X1. With the likes of Rio Ferdinand and Wes Brown maturing into excellent defenders, and Gareth Southgate still on the scene, competition is stiff.

The towering presence at the back in the last World Cup.

Emile Heskey

Emile Heskey

Birthplace: Leicester, 11 January 1978

Nickname: Bruno

England debut: 9.6.99 against Bulgaria

Height: 6ft 1in   Weight: 13.0st

Signed for Liverpool from Leicester City for £11m

Liverpool's most expensive transfer player

Power and presence

Many eyebrows were raised when Gerard Houllier paid Leicester City a record £11 million to bring Emile Heskey to Anfield in March 2000. It was a lot to pay for a player who was nowhere near the finished article.

Houllier knew he was buying sure-fire potential, and he wanted Liverpool to be the place where Heskey's prodigious talent blossomed. For eighteen months, Houllier's team selection suggested that he felt the Heskey-Owen partnership offered the greatest promise. Heskey's power and physical presence was a perfect foil for Owen. And 22 goals in 2000-01 - his first full season at Liverpool - represented an impressive goal return. At the end of that glorious year - which yielded five trophies - many Liverpool fans said that "Bruno" had made a bright start to his Anfield career.

Key squad member

Kevin Keegan handed Heskey his first senior cap in February 2000, in a friendly against Argentina. It is a testament to the strides he has made that he is now seen as a key member of Sven-Goran Eriksson's squad. Like Houllier, Eriksson seems to favour the Heskey-Owen combination as his first-choice strike partnership.

This summer will be his sternest test yet, as he tries to impose himself on the best defenders in the world and help fire England to World Cup glory.

Nick Barmby

Breakthrough on the left

The left side of midfield has proved to be the thorniest problem for England's managers in recent years. Many players have been tried there, but Nick Barmby looks favourite to start in that position when the serious business gets under way in Japan and Korea - providing he can regain his fitness. Last October, it was confirmed that he needed an ankle operation which would keep him out until the new year. It must have been a huge blow to Barmby, who had been in such good form since joining Liverpool in the summer of 2000 from rivals Everton for £6 million.

With his £6 million move to Anfield, Barmby finally achieved what he had first attempted ten years earlier. He had a two-week trial at Liverpool as a teenager, but failed to make an impression. Spurs took him on instead, and it was at White Hart Lane that he made his mark as one of the brightest young talents in the land. At 18, he broke into Ossie Ardiles's flamboyant, attacking Spurs team, playing alongside Teddy Sheringham, Darren Anderton and Jurgen Klinsmann.

Scintillating performances

During the 1999-2000 season, he strung together a run of scintillating performances which earned him a recall to the England squad, after four years in the international wilderness. A couple of appearances followed in the ill-fated Euro 2000 campaign. It was immediately after that tournament that he left Goodison for Anfield, becoming the first Everton player for over 40 years to swap the blue shirt for the red of their arch-rivals.

At White Hart Lane he made his mark as one of the brightest young talents in the land.

Nick Barmby

Birthplace: Hull 11 February 1974

Height: 5ft 7in Weight: 11st.3lb

Club: Liverpool FC

Previous Clubs :Tottenham Hotspur, Middlesbrough, Everton

England debut: March 1995

Ashley Cole

Meteoric rise

The phrase "meteoric rise" might have been invented for Ashley Cole. His progress from third-choice left-back for Arsenal to international player has come at a dizzying speed. Perhaps he has been rather fortunate in that England are not blessed with too many left-sided defenders. However, Cole has pushed himself to the fore, both for club and country, with some classy performances over the past season and a half.

A product of Arsenal's Centre of Excellence, Cole started out as a striker before establishing himself at left back. His old attacking instincts are there for all to see, though. He takes every opportunity to get forward, and his searing pace means that he can turn defence into attack very quickly, something which is very important in the modern game. There have been the occasional defensive lapses, and at 21 he is not yet the finished article. But where better to learn his trade than Highbury, home of the meanest defence of the past decade?

International debut

Cole soon had even more reason to pinch himself. In February 2001, with just a handful of Premiership games for Arsenal to his name, he was called up to the senior England squad by the new England manager. He didn't get on in the match, a friendly against Spain which England won 3-0. Michael Ball and Chris Powell each played 45 minutes at left back that day. His debut came a month later, in the World Cup qualifier in Albania, and with every international game since he has cemented his place in the squad.

He takes every opportunity to get forward, and his searing pace means that he can turn defence into attack very quickly.

Ashley Cole

Birthplace: Stepney, 20 December 1980

Height: 5ft 8in

Weight: 10st 7lb

England debut: v. Albania in March 2001

Club: Arsenal

Gary Neville

Gary Neville

Birthplace: born 18 February 1975
Height: 5ft 10in · Weight: 12st 8lb
England debut: 3.6.95 v Japan
Club: Manchester Utd

Tackling back

Gary Neville made his debut for United in 1994, when he was 19. Paul Parker was the established right back at the time, both for United and England. Neville soon stepped into Parker's boots in both teams. His international call-up came in June 1995 against Japan. He had played just 19 first-team games at the time, a postwar record. For almost eight years he has been a key member of the side which has dominated domestic football, and his mantelpiece must be creaking under the weight of the medals he has won. Indeed, with a string of Premiership titles and FA Cup wins under his belt, not to mention that glorious European Champions Cup victory in 1999, there is little more for Neville to achieve at club level. He has already done more in the game than most players dream of, and with his 27th birthday coming up, he is only just approaching his prime.

Fiercely patriotic

As far as international football is concerned, Neville has much greater scope to build on his considerable achievements. He missed out on Euro 96, was part of Glenn Hoddle's squad which went out in the second round in France '98, and was involved in the disappointing Euro 2000 campaign. Getting to the latter stages of a World Cup must rank high among his remaining footballing ambitions. He is famously tight-lipped when the national anthem strikes up before an England match, but Neville is fiercely patriotic. He simply prefers to prepare for the big games in quiet contemplation.

Neville's understanding with David Beckham gives England a potent attacking option down the right flank, and the likes of Danny Mills and Jamie Carragher will have to play well if they want that England No 2 shirt.

Neville's understanding with David Beckham gives England a potent attacking option down the right flank.

Wes Brown

"The new Bobby Moore"

It is always hard for an exciting young player when he is compared to one of the greats of the past. When it's World Cup year and you've been dubbed "the new Bobby Moore", the hype and pressure can become excessive. Fortunately, Wes Brown is an unflappable, phlegmatic character and takes it all in his stride. In fact, those are some of the qualities which have prompted comparisons with England's World Cup winning captain of 1966. Brown also has all the hallmarks that made Moore such a great player. He is an excellent reader of the game, times his tackles to perfection and is totally at ease in possession. Add to that the fact that the United youngster is quicker than Moore was and better in the air, and it is easy to see why he is so highly regarded.

Long future

Alex Ferguson's controversial decision to let Stam go last autumn must go down, at least in part, as a compliment to Brown. Laurent Blanc was bought as an immediate stop-gap, but Brown is obviously seen as the man with a long future ahead of him at Old Trafford.

Rio Ferdinand attracted all the headlines with his £18 million move from West Ham to Leeds just over a year ago. Given that benchmark, what Brown would fetch on the transfer market today is anybody's guess.

With only 11 appearances in a United shirt to his name when he turned out against Hungary in 1999, Brown became the fastest-ever capped player.

Gareth Southgate

Gareth Southgate

Birthplace: 3 September 1970, Watford

Height: 6ft 0in **Weight:** 12st 3lb

England debut: 12.12.95 v. Portugal

Club: Middlesbrough

Signed for Crystal Palace from trainee.

Culture at the back

Gareth Southgate is one of those unfortunate players who, no matter what they achieve in the game, will always be remembered for one dramatic moment of failure. His penalty shoot-out miss against Germany in the semi-final of Euro '96 hit all England fans hard. The team was on a roll and playing well; "Football's Coming Home" blared out from the stands; there was a widespread feeling that victory against the old enemy was on the cards. After his tamely-struck spot kick was saved, Southgate's face mirrored the disappointment of the country. To his credit, Southgate went on to poke fun at himself by appearing in a celebrated pizza advertisement, where he was joined by other notable members of the "penalty missers' club".

Youngest captain

Watford-born Southgate made his name at Crystal Palace almost a decade ago, when he was the youngest captain in the Premiership. In 1995, Aston Villa paid £2.5 million to bring him to the Midlands. He had often played in midfield for Palace; it was at Villa that he established himself as one of the country's most cultured central defenders.

He was a key member of Glenn Hoddle's squad at France '98, and also featured in Euro 2000. Southgate was nearly 30 when he joined up with Kevin Keegan's squad for the latter tournament. When that adventure ended - so disappointingly - it seemed that his international days might be numbered. There was a crop of talented young defenders coming through, and it looked the right time to build for the future.

His £6.5 million move to Middlesbrough in July 2001 has given him a new lease of life, however, and his performances have earned him a recall to the England squad.

He now looks to be a strong contender for a place in Sven-Goran Eriksson's starting XI when the serious World Cup business gets under way.

Robbie Fowler

The Poacher

Robbie Fowler dislikes ranking the many goals he has scored in his nine years in top-flight football. There have been plenty of spectacular strikes in that time, but the poacher's goals bring him just as much pleasure. He is widely regarded by his fellow professionals as the best finisher in the business.

30-goal mark

Fowler opened his account for Liverpool in his very first game, a League Cup tie away to Fulham in September 1993. He followed it up by scoring all five in a 5-0 win in the return match at Anfield. He fired a highly creditable 18 goals in that debut season, but it was during the following three years that he hit top gear. He passed the 30-goal mark in each of those campaigns, firmly establishing himself as the natural successor to the great Ian Rush.

His scoring form earned him his first senior England cap in 1996. He made the squad for Euro 96, but Shearer and Sheringham were in such sparkling form that he only managed a brief substitute's appearance against Spain. He was also unlucky when France '98 came round, having sustained a bad knee injury in February of that year.

Both Gerard Houllier and Sven-Goran Eriksson seemed to regard the Heskey-Owen partnership as the dream striking ticket. Fowler hit back with a terrific goal in the Worthington Cup Final against Birmingham. He then came on as substitute in both the FA and UEFA Cup Finals. He grabbed Liverpool's fourth goal in that memorable clash with Alaves.

Fowler's controversial move to Leeds could provide the boost he needs for a place in the England starting XI in June.

He is widely regarded by his fellow professionals as the best finisher in the business.

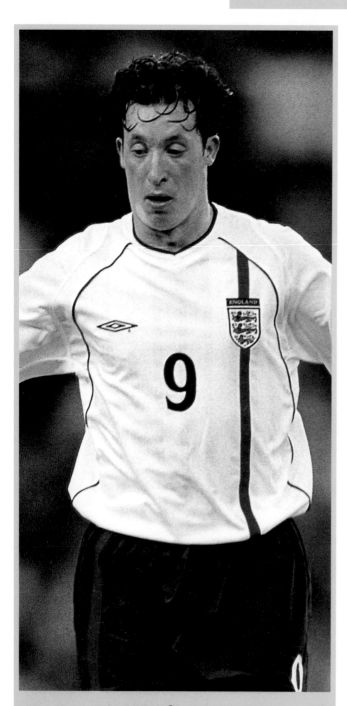

Robbie Fowler

Birthplace: Toxteth, Liverpool 9 April 1975

England debut: 27.3.96 v. Bulgaria

Height: 5ft 11in   Weight: 11st 10lb

Club: Leeds United

Signed for Leeds Utd for £11m in November 2001.

The Young Player of the Year in both 1995 and 1996

Steve McManaman

Steve McManaman

Birthplace: Bootle, 11 February 1972

Position: Midfielder

Height: 6in 0ft Weight: 10st 6lbs

England debut: 16.11.94 v. Nigeria

Club: Real Madrid (Spain)

Previous Clubs: Signed for Liverpool 1990, left on a free transfer in 1999.

Natural flair

When 27-year-old McManaman decided he needed a fresh challenge in the summer of 1999, after 16 years at Liverpool, he chose to join Real Madrid on a free transfer under the Bosman ruling.

Even at 29, McManaman continues to divide opinion among pundits and fans. Critics say he is a luxury player who has failed to reproduce his best club form when he has turned out for England. Macca fans point to his superb performances at Euro 96, where Terry Venables gave him a much freer role. McManaman is at his best when he is running at defenders at pace. He hasn't always been given the freedom to express himself; too often he has been played out on the left wing, with defensive duties too. That's when he has been least effective.

Spectacular strike

McManaman's career at Real looked to be over before it had really started when a new manager took over soon after he joined the club. Macca was told he had no future there, but he dug in and proved his worth. By the end of his debut season, not only had he forced his way into the first team, but also helped Real to reach the Champions League Final. He capped it with a spectacular strike in the 3-0 win over Valencia. After nearly three years in the Primera Liga, where the technical and tactical side of the game is so advanced, McManaman is certainly a better all-round player.

If he can combine the best of the Spanish game with the natural flair that made him such a favourite at Anfield, his best England days could still be ahead of him.

Teddy Sheringham

The perfect striking partner

Teddy Sheringham

Birthplace: Walthamstow, 2 April 1966

Height: 6ft 0in **Weight:** 12st 3lb

England debut v. Poland in 1993

Club: Tottenham Hotspur

Teddy was already the wrong side of 30 when Alex Ferguson brought him to Old Trafford to fill Eric Cantona's boots. He struggled to win a regular place, initially, and with the likes of Cole, Yorke and Solskjaer at Ferguson's disposal, competition was fierce. Sheringham bounced back to play a vital part in the run-in to the glorious 1998-99 campaign. After helping United to secure yet another Premiership title, he came off the bench in the FA Cup Final to score one and make another for Scholes - a performance which won him the Man of the Match award. Then, most dramatically of all, he came on as a late substitute in the Champions Cup Final against Bayern Munich and turned the game on its head. He scored one and laid on the winner for Solskjaer, a goal which made United champions of Europe once again.

Terrific form

Last season he showed that you write him off at your peril. He was in sparkling form, scored 22 goals in all competitions and won both the Football Writers and the PFA Player of the Year awards. Sven-Goran Eriksson recognised Sheringham's terrific form by recalling him to the international squad for his first match in charge, against Spain in February 2001.

The end of last season saw Sheringham back at his beloved Tottenham. Glenn Hoddle knew that even at 35, Sheringham would be a major asset in his rebuilding job at White Hart Lane. He was a substitute for that dramatic clash with Greece last October, when England badly under-performed and scored with a delightful header just seconds after joining the action. Sheringham looks unlikely to start for England this summer, but his happy knack of coming off the bench to influence the outcome of games could be an excellent weapon in Eriksson's armoury.

Sheringham has the ability to drop deep and play his twin-striker in with deft flicks and slide-rule passes.

David Seaman

David Seaman

Birthplace: Rotherham, 19 September 1963

Height: 6' 4"

Weight: 14st 8lb

Club: Arsenal

England debut: 1988 Saudi Arabia

England's rock

David Seaman won't be far short of his 39th birthday when England head out to Japan and Korea this summer. The good news for England fans is that he is a mere stripling compared to some 'keepers who have graced the final stages of the World Cup. Peter Shilton had turned 40 when he played in the semi-final defeat by Germany at Italia '90; and the great Dino Zoff had also reached that milestone when he captained Italy to victory in Spain '82. Also, no one has yet done enough to wrest Seaman's England jersey from him. In fact, the battle for the goalkeeping spot looks likely to be between the Arsenal man and another veteran, Nigel Martyn.

Illustrious career

Seaman's illustrious career began at Martyn's club, Leeds United. He moved on to Peterborough, but it was after he joined Birmingham City, in 1984, that he began to make a name for himself. When QPR came in for him in August 1986, they had to stump up £225,000, more than twice the amount the Blues had paid for him.

It was during his four-year stay at Loftus Road that Seaman made his England debut, in a 1-1 draw against Saudi Arabia in November 1988. Two years later, Arsenal made him the most expensive 'keeper in Britain when they paid £1.3 million to bring him to Highbury.

For nearly 12 years Seaman has been part of a defensive unit that has been the envy of the country. He has been a rock for England over the same period. Who can forget his penalty heroics against Scotland and Spain at Euro 96? Six years on, Richard Wright is threatening Seaman's Arsenal place, but it would be a brave punter who would bet against Seaman being between the sticks for England this summer.

No one has yet done enough to wrest Seaman's England jersey from him.

Pace and power

Cole began his career at Arsenal. He found opportunities at Highbury limited, a situation that wasn't helped by the fact that George Graham apparently rated Kevin Campbell a better prospect. Cole was sold to Bristol City in 1992 for just £500,000. Twenty goals in 41 games at Ashton Gate was the kind of record that was bound to attract attention, and Newcastle came in for him in March 1993. The £1.75 million represented good business for Bristol City, but Newcastle certainly got a bargain.

Cole immediately started banging in the goals for the Tyneside club at a phenomenal rate, helping them to win promotion to the Premiership in his first season. Cole and Peter Beardsley spearheaded an attractive, attacking side, and the pairing proved equally effective when Newcastle stepped up to the top flight.

Improving fortunes

The goals and trophies came thick and fast in Cole's seven years at Old Trafford. But it was no surprise when Hoddle, who criticised Cole for needing too many chances before putting one away, overlooked him for France '98. To his credit, he got his head down and carried on doing his stuff at club level. His international fortunes looked to have improved when his old club boss, Kevin Keegan, replaced Hoddle in the England job. Keegan's reign was short-lived, though, as England got off to a shaky start in qualifying for the 2002 World Cup. Sven-Goran Eriksson came in with a clean slate, prepared to give each player his chance. Cole responded by finally breaking his international scoring duck. It had taken 13 matches for him to get off the mark, hardly the kind of record to make the world sit up and take notice. Even so, the fact remains that Cole has been a key figure in United's success over recent years. Cole will hope that his move to Blackburn and the opportunity of playing every week will put him in the front line for World Cup first-team selection.

Andrew Cole

Birthplace: Nottingham 15 October 1971

Height: 5ft 10in

Weight: 12st 4lb

Club: Blackburn Rovers

England debut: January 1995

A striker who can overtake the great Denis Law as United's top scorer in European competition must have lots to offer England.

Nigel Martyn

Nigel Martyn

Birthplace: St Austell, Cornwall, 11 August 1966

Height: 6ft 2in

Weight: 14st 8lb

England debut: 12.5.92 Against Hungary

Club: Leeds United

First £1 million goalkeeper when Crystal Palace signed him from Bristol Rovers in 1989 at 23.

Shot-stopper

Almost inevitably, it was David Beckham's stunning last-gasp free-kick against Greece last October that grabbed all the headlines. It is the goal that carried England to the World Cup finals that will be replayed endlessly and live long in the memory. However, Nigel Martyn played an equally important part in saving - quite literally - England from having to go into the play-offs. He made two brilliant saves to prevent Greece from going two goals in front. He kept a side which was performing poorly in the game, and effectively created the platform for Beckham to work his magic.

Learning the trade

Although they are of veteran status, both Martyn and Seaman are class acts, so it could come down to who the form player is in the run-up to the tournament to decide who gets the 'keeper's jersey. Martyn signed for Leeds on the eve of his 30th birthday, in July 1996. The Cornishman had already enjoyed long and illustrious spells at Bristol Rovers and Crystal Palace. He had nearly 400 league appearances under his belt by the time he went to Elland Road. Having spent a long time learning his trade at these lesser lights of the footballing world, Martyn was desperate for top club honours - and to unseat Seaman as England's established No 1.

He started superbly at Leeds, winning the club's Player of the Year award in his debut season. This season he looks as good as ever. His mature, commanding performances have given the defence confidence and authority. The young lions further upfield get a lot of the attention, but it is Martyn at the heart of a resilient defensive unit which has been just as important in the rise of David O'Leary's team.

Martyn cost Leeds £2.25 million, breaking the record held by David Seaman. Having spent so many years in the Arsenal man's shadow, Martyn would love to displace him again - this time on the pitch at the World Cup.

He kept an England side which was performing poorly in the game, and effectively created the platform for Beckham to work his magic.

Sven's England

"The standard is high and the future is very good for England"

When Sven-Goran Eriksson took over as manager of England, making him the tenth permanent manager over the last fifty years, it was the most controversial appointment the national team had ever made. Many thought that the job should be done by an Englishman while others that it should be given to the man most likely to bring the success that the fans were demanding.

Sven's pedigree was beyond doubt. He had enjoyed much recent success in the Italian league having guided Lazio to the "double" in the 1999-2000 season.

His knowledge of the English game was limited, so he set about an arduous tour of the country to get more of an appreciation of the players available. There was little time to settle in with England's final and crucial qualifying games just months away.

England's Managers

1946-62	Walter Winterbottom
1963-74	Alf Ramsey
1974-77	Don Revie
1977-82	Ron Greenwood
1982-90	Bobby Robson
!990-93	Graham Taylor
1994-96	Terry Venables
1996-99	Glenn Hoddle
!999-2000	Kevin Keegan
2000 -	Sven-Goran Eriksson

Within his first year as manager and in a precarious group position when he took over, Eriksson's England qualified as group winners with the highlight that resounding 5-1 victory over Germany.

This is a Parragon Book
First published in 2002

Parragon, Queen Street House, 4 Queen Street, Bath BA1 1HE, UK.

Copyright ©Parragon 2002
All Photographs copyright Getty Images

ISBN Hardback: 0-75258-362-X

Conceived, designed and produced by
Atlantic Publishing, London

Acknowledgments
This book would not have been possible without the help of
Rick Mayston and Matt Stevens

Thanks also to Steve Torrington, Dave Sheppard, Brian Jackson, Alan Pinnock,
Peter Wright, Trevor Bunting, Simon Taylor, Sheila Harding, Christine Hoy, Maureen Hill,
Anthony Linden, Carol and Cliff Salter, Tom and Harry Nettleton.

Designed by: John Dunne
Pre press by Croxsons
Printed in Dubai